THE DOLLARS AND CENTS OF STARTING YOUR SMALL FARM OR HOMESTEAD

A Decision-Making Workbook and Planning Guide
WITH FREE PLANNING WORKSHEETS AND RESOURCES

© 2020 Jamie Oliver

Published by:
The Lowe Farm
17473 Longview Dr
Smithfield VA 23430
www.thelowefarm.com

First Print Edition: 2020

Published in the United States of America

All rights reserved. For Personal Use Only. No portion of this book may be reproduced in any form without permission from the publisher, except as permitted by U.S. copyright law. Cover image and all publication images belong to Jamie Oliver and The Lowe Farm. No images in this publication may be used without specific written permission of the owner.

For permissions contact:
Jamie Oliver
thelowefarm@gmail.com

Connect with the Author on Facebook: facebook.com/walkinginhighcotton
Visit the Author's website: walkinginhighcotton.com

TABLE OF CONTENTS

INTRODUCTION: IS RAISING YOUR OWN MEAT REALLY FRUGAL? 6

CHAPTER ONE: THE DOLLARS AND CENTS OF STARTING YOUR SMALL FARM OR HOMESTEAD 8

    1. Know Your Purpose 8

    2. Compare Apples to Apples 9

    3. Be Brave and Keep Learning 10

    4. Filter Opinions 10

    5. Have an Exit Strategy 11

CHAPTER TWO: FINDING LAND FOR YOUR SMALL FARM OR HOMESTEAD 13

    1. You Can Farm WITHOUT Owning Land 13

    2. You Can Start SMALL 14

    3. You WILL Change Your Mind 14

    4. There's No Such Thing as a Blank Canvas 14

    5. Something's Better Than Nothing 15

    6. Know What You're Looking For 15

    7. Know What You're Looking At 15

    8. Look for Your Community 16

    9. Check Land Uses 16

    10. Think Long-Term 17

CHAPTER THREE: BUILDINGS AND SHELTERS ON YOUR SMALL FARM OR HOMESTEAD 19

    1. What Is the Building's Purpose? 20

    2. Does It Need to Be Mobile? 21

    3. What Else Do You Need Storage For? 21

    4. Are You Sure It Should Go *There*? 21

    5. Are You Following Your Own Work Patterns? 22

    6. Is This Design Practical? 22

7. Can It Be Expanded? 23

8. Are You Reinventing the Wheel for No Reason? 23

9. Do You Already Have Something You Can Use? 23

10. Do You Care How It Looks? 24

CHAPTER FOUR: FOOD AND WATER ON YOUR SMALL FARM OR HOMESTEAD 26

Grass 26

Hay 27

Grain 28

Water 29

CHAPTER FIVE: HEALTH AND WELLNESS ON YOUR SMALL FARM OR HOMESTEAD 31

1. Create a Healthy Environment 31

2. Match Your Animals to Your Environment 32

3. Create a Routine for Preventative Health Care 33

4. Provide for Expert Help When Needed 34

CHAPTER SIX: CHOOSING LIVESTOCK FOR YOUR SMALL FARM OR HOMESTEAD 36

Are You Ready for Livestock on Your Farm? 36

What Type of Livestock Should You Have on Your Farm? 41

What Specific Breed of Livestock Should You Have on Your Farm? 45

CHAPTER SEVEN: YOUR SMALL FARM OR HOMESTEAD GARAGE 49

What Do You Need to Have? 49

Where Do You Get What You Need? 50

Where Do You Put What You Get? 51

CHAPTER EIGHT: ORGANIZING YOUR FARM RECORDS 53

Why Use a Digital Calendar Instead of Spreadsheets or Paper? 53

What Farm Information Can You Track Using Google Calendar? 54

How Do You Track Farm Records in Google Calendar? 55

How Do You Use the SEARCH Feature in Google Calendar? 55

CHAPTER 9: FINDING UNEXPECTED GOODNESS ON THE FARM 58

REFERENCES 60

WORKSHEETS 61
   1. Finding Land for Your Small Farm 61
   2. Assessing Land and Community Around Your Small Farm 61
   3. Buildings and Shelters for Your Small Farm 61
   4. When to Call the Vet at Your Small Farm 61
   5. Farm Visit Notes 61
   6. Choosing Livestock for Your Small Farm 61
   7. Assessing Livestock Breeds for Your Small Farm 61

INTRODUCTION: IS RAISING YOUR OWN MEAT REALLY FRUGAL?

I read an article recently about how cheap it is to raise your own meat in your backyard, and I must admit, it hit me all wrong.

I love homesteading and I love our small farm life. I would never want to discourage *anyone* from trying it. But I also don't think it helps anyone be successful to make it all sound easy-peasy, like you can just throw some animals in your backyard and suddenly you have organic food for a quarter of the price of the grocery store. That's not how it works.

Frugal is usually defined as some version of *economically sparing*, *thrifty*, *inexpensive*, *careful of costs*, or *prudent in fiscal decisions*. Here's the problem with a lot of homesteading "costs" people put on the web--the only numbers you're seeing are short-term, hard operating costs. How much did the animal, it's feed, water, and medicine cost for one year? Everything else is lumped under "start-up costs" or not counted because it didn't come up yet. Some costs are not consistent if you haven't been doing it very long. Most things don't have to be replaced every single year but are required every few years. So how can you make "prudent fiscal decisions" if you're not being realistic?

We have watched so many people get started...and quit...because after a few years it's just not what they expected. Long-term livestock farming, even on a small-scale, is challenging. Fiscally and emotionally. Giving people the impression that it's *cheap and easy* sets them up for failure.

We've had folks off-load unwanted sheep, goats, chickens, and even a horse on us. Raising livestock is not a frugal endeavor in and of itself. The *real* dollars and cents of raising your own meat is rarely less than buying from the grocery store unless you take *out* all the start-up costs, land and labor costs, and emotional costs. It is a rare farm that is making a mortgage payment by selling goat-milk soap at the local farmers' market.

So, if the numbers are always bad, why farm?

Well, there *are* good reasons for raising your own food. And there are some good ways to avoid costly mistakes and mitigate your on-going expenses. It can be *affordable*, if not frugal. I don't want to stop anyone--I'd love to see everyone raising their own food! But it needs to be done with realistic expectations and practical thoughtfulness to be sustainable and successful.

Some *good* reasons to raise animals?

Having animals is fun!

They force you into a mode of self-discipline far beyond anything you'll ever feel for a vegetable garden.

They provide quality food for your table and teach you sufficiency skills that can't be valued.

They make you laugh!

They teach you about life and death in a visceral way that cannot be replaced.

They are an important part of a healthy ecosystem if you want to be a good land steward.

If you're going down this small farm and homestead path for any of these *good* reasons, there are ways to be *more* frugal about it.

Let's talk about the *real* costs of this lifestyle, and ways to reduce them. Let's discuss where to make wise cuts and where you can't afford to be unprepared. Let's talk about the expensive mistakes we made so you can avoid them! I've included several planning workbook pages to help you take your own notes as you explore and plan out this amazing dream of homesteading!

****

CHAPTER ONE: THE DOLLARS AND CENTS OF STARTING YOUR SMALL FARM OR HOMESTEAD

When I posted on our blog, Walking in High Cotton, that raising your own meat is not really *frugal*, a lot of folks agreed, and said farming is *not cheap*. The grocery store prices give the average shopper a skewed idea of the actual costs of farming.

But some readers disagreed and said that *frugal* and *cheap* are not the same thing. Their argument was that in the long-term the intangible benefits make it a frugal choice regardless of the up-front costs. The idea of quality vs quantity.

I think both are right.

It's expensive. But it has priceless long-term benefits. And small farms can make careful choices to keep costs down and bring income in.

The purpose of this workbook is to walk through the key cost areas of starting a small livestock farm or homestead and help you do some hard thinking about your hows and whys *before* you bring animals out to your place. It is not meant to be a business plan! Actual costs vary widely from place-to-place, and most are completely dependent on decisions that you, the farmer, make for your farm system.

The worksheets you'll find here are to help you take notes, compare options, and do some practical thinking to frame a realistic fiscal strategy for your farm and give you a decision-making framework as you move forward.

To start with, here are 5 basis points to sort out for yourself.

1. Know Your Purpose

Are you *homesteading*? Meaning just focused on raising your own food and being self-sufficient?

Are you a *small farm*? Raising your own food *and* food specifically for commercial sale?

Are you more interested in being a *cottage industry*? Meaning your real purpose is not food, but the by-products from animals such as raising your sheep for the wool and creating the wool products on your homestead?

You don't have to use my terms or definitions; the point is that you sit down and define what you're doing for *yourself*. If you want the farm to pay for itself, you'll have a much different decision-making strategy than if you're doing it as a semi-productive hobby and your mortgage is paid from an off-farm job.

Write down some general goals, some basic boundaries, to get started. It's not uncommon to lose yourself in the moment when walking past the fluffy yellow chicks at Tractor Supply. Sometimes reminding yourself that you only bring edibles to the barnyard can cool your impulsiveness.

2. Compare Apples to Apples

This is probably our biggest challenge area! You see what someone else is doing, and it seems like it's working great, and you just want to do *that*. But it doesn't work like that for you and you end up disappointed and discouraged. So often, you must look past the surface of a farm and give hard attention to the underlying *system* they're working with.

Do they have someone home at the farm full-time? That's completely different then a situation where the owner works off-farm full-time.

Do they do all their lambing in the barn? If you plan to lamb mostly on pasture that's a totally different system!

Do they have a beautiful, predator-proof chicken coop with hardware cloth, sand flooring, and cinderblock foundation? That's completely different than a philosophy of everything being mobile and having a free-range flock.

Animals act differently, produce differently, and grow differently in different systems, different climates, and different routines. You can learn from anyone but be careful when you're comparing methods to decide that you're really comparing apples to apples. You'll save yourself a lot of frustration.

3. Be Brave and Keep Learning

This one's for all my fellow booklovers, planners, researchers, and Type A friends.

You don't have to (you can't possibly!) know everything before you start. Sometimes you just have to dive in. You're going to make mistakes. You're going to change your mind. Things are going to go better than expected and worse than expected. The key is to keep learning and try not to make the same mistake twice!

A lot of times after giving a talk or a farm tour, we hear some version of "Well, you grew up on a farm, right?" Nope. Neither of us grew up on a full-time livestock farm. We learned on the go. We learned in school. We learned from other farmers around us. We learned from books and YouTube. And some things you're only going to learn by getting out there and doing it! At some point you have to be brave and start doing it!

And when it starts to feel too familiar or boring, there's always a new skill to learn. A new project to tackle. A new ideal to investigate. Honestly, I'm usually more overwhelmed by how much there is still to be learned than I am ever bored or thinking I've got it all figured out.

4. Filter Opinions

People find this farming, homesteading, livestock-raising lifestyle fascinating. Disturbing. Dirty. Loud. Confusing. Upsetting. Beautiful. Peaceful. {snort} CRAZY.

You're going to run into so many opinions about what you're doing. Some will be nice and some not-so-nice. Some helpful and constructive, some just plain ignorant. You learn to grow a thick skin and filter the opinions coming in at you, so you don't get distracted by every new idea or discouraged by naysayers.

Start by reminding yourself about your purpose. If your purpose is to raise animals for your own food, then you might not put too much stock in a vegetarian's opinion of your processing operation.

Then ask yourself if they're comparing apples to apples. If you're trying to run an organic, grass-based operation, you might want to brush off criticism from your local feed-lot operators. They're working a system TOTALLY different than yours.

And then remember that you're still learning. We're *all* still learning! Always be open-minded, but don't be fooled into getting discouraged by opposing voices. Weed through the words, take what's helpful, and toss the rest.

5. Have an Exit Strategy

This sounds horrible, but it's so important! I'm not just talking about exiting THE FARM in whole. I'm talking about having a strategy for each of the different enterprises you'll find yourself involved in. This lifestyle is not easy, and farming is an extremely diverse field. There is NO REASON to keep up with enterprises you don't enjoy. Before you get into any farm venture, know what your exit strategy is if it doesn't work out the way you expect.

Say you buy goats and they're a pain in the neck and you can't keep them fenced and it turns out you don't *like* goat milk...

Have an exit strategy to re-coup your investment and get out of it. Try something else instead.

Here's 2 simple tips we try to follow to keep our exit options open.

Only try something you're willing to eat!

That way no matter what happens, you'll be able to get something out of it. Folks ask why we don't have any alpacas. Well, we don't eat alpacas. What would we do with them if we couldn't sell the fiber? We also don't eat goat or drink goat's milk, so for us goats are a no-go. If we get stuck with unsold lamb or beef at the end of the season, we're still ok because we're just stocking our own freezer and cutting our own grocery bill.

Always start small!

If you end up allergic to goat milk, it's much easier to re-sell your dairy goats if you only have one or two. It's much harder to get out if you with a whole herd! Your first go at processing your own pastured broilers? Start with one pen of 25 birds. Don't invest in building 3 pens and ordering 150 birds your first batch. Not everyone can handle the butchering process.

And take the time to understand what "small" is. Everyone wants a *few* chickens to raise their own eggs and don't realize that 5 hens can mean 2-3 dozen eggs *a week* in the summer!

To have any sense of success, farming must be a long-term choice. And it must be made for all those reasons you can never put into words.

Because there will be a lot of days when you don't have success by any worldly measure.

Not from the bottom line at the bank.

Not from appreciation from your customers.

Not from understanding from your family.

You might have neighbors complaining about the noise at weaning time. Or about the roosters at dawn. Or about seeing you processing meat in the garage. There will be dark winter mornings when every water bucket on the farm is frozen, the sheep try to eat you, a weasel breaks in and kills half your flock of chickens, or you have to be out doing chores in a hurricane.

And sometimes there are no dollars and cents when it comes to finding new babies in the grass, or coffee at sunrise, or crazy snuggling chickens.

****

CHAPTER TWO: FINDING LAND FOR YOUR SMALL FARM OR HOMESTEAD

In the back of our minds, I think all of us small-farm-minded folks have an Old MacDonald, Little Patch O'Heaven, green pastures and babbling brooks, daydream going on when we first envision *our* place. Or maybe it's wide open prairies with clear blue skies and rugged, snow-capped peaks in the background. Either way, it's beautiful. It's perfect. It's everything we ever imagined.

And when push comes to shove, it's expensive.

Farming begins and ends with *land*, and these days land is hard to come by. Even if someone was to walk up and hand you the deed, property taxes have run a lot of folks right off the old home place. Around here we call it *land rich and cash poor*. You inherit land that's not mortgaged but struggle to pay the taxes and keep up the maintenance. Real estate is only an "investment" if you can make money *on it* or *sell it*. And most farm-minded people don't want to sell. We want to find, buy, and keep.

Here's 10 important things to keep in mind when you're looking for land to farm.

1. You Can Farm WITHOUT Owning Land

No one starts out thinking this way, but it's true and it's important to think about.

You can farm on rented land--pretty much every modern commercial farm is more than 50% rental property. The schedule F (Farm Income) tax forms have an entire category devoted to rents. And a lot of modern homesteaders get started on rental property and hope to eventually move to their *own* piece of property. And if you rent, your costs might be tax deductible and you don't have to pay real estate taxes!

When we first got out of college and got married, we rented an old house on a working dairy farm. We had nothing to do with the farm, technically, but helped the farm family here and there, did some relief milking for them to go on vacation, and helped some other neighbors move sheep occasionally. Without having a farm at all we picked up a lot of helpful experience just by having a willing spirit!

It's just best to break free of the "buying" mindset when you're starting out. If you wait until you can afford the "perfect" piece of property, you'll never get started. Start where you are and, as you see in later chapters, a lot of your farm "infrastructure" can move with you later. If you plan right.

2. You Can Start SMALL

Mini-farming and Square Foot Gardening are common small-ground production methods. You can start gardening right on your apartment patio. Don't get your mind locked on land, when you could be investing in *skills*, while saving up for land. Inexperience can cost you a lot more in the long run than land will.

No matter what property you're working with, you can still be growing your skills so you're ready for your "perfect" farm.

3. You WILL Change Your Mind

I talked about this a little bit in the section on exit strategies. You might think you need 20 acres because you're going be a cattle farmer--then it turns out you hate cows. It's not a crime. There's plenty of other ways to farm, other livestock to be enjoyed, other meaningful work to be done. But if you bought your land thinking you know exactly what your future will hold, you might have made a mistake.

Keep an open mind for *all* the possibilities of a piece of property. Who knows what you'll be interested in 15 years down the line—or what your children will want to explore as their contribution to the farm! Be sure that you're sorting the land features into categories of what *can be changed*, what *cannot be changed*, and what will *take a lot of work and money to be changed*.

4. There's No Such Thing as a Blank Canvas

All land has a history. Whether it's been used, abused, loved, ignored...the soil has a history that you should probably investigate. What's been on that property for the last 50 years?

I've seen farms that have hidden dump sites, farms that have old drainage tile that turns into sink holes, farms that have unknown water wells and septic fields. Take plenty of time to research your property through multiple sources to find out about it before committing. Not everything shows up right away.

5. Something's Better Than Nothing

We all have visions of magnificent barns, miles and miles of board fence, and a neat little tractor shed full of shiny implements. If we're lucky enough to even *find* such a place, the price tag is enough to make a small farmer cry.

When we do find something we can afford, it usually includes a ramshackle pile of half-rotten wood and rusted tin that they call a barn; a rusted-out mower held together with baling twine and duct tape; and miles of broken barb-wire fence on spindly cedar posts.

The truth is that, just like the pasture, starting with *something* is better than starting from scratch. Even if it just ends ups a heap of scrap wood for future projects, you'll find a use for it. To be a thrifty small farmer you have to find ways to use *everything*.

6. Know What You're Looking For

Make a wish list. Get it all out. Then sit down and decide what on the list is and is *not* negotiable. Think in terms of quality of life issues, not farm products (remember, you might change your mind!). Do you want beautiful sunsets? Do you want peace and quiet? Do you care if you're by a road? Do you want running water? Timber? Wildlife? You can change what kind of shed you have or how much is pasture and how much is timber or where the garden is...but you can't change having a creek or being next to a road. Also keep in mind that you're going to need a lot of water for livestock. Whether it's watering your garden or your cows, if you're on public water it's going to be expensive!

7. Know What You're Looking At

Understand the area you're moving into.

Are you moving into an area that is currently rural? Will you have access to feed stores, a veterinarian, and understanding neighbors? Is your area growing? Are you going to be next to an industrial park in 10 years, or a subdivision? Do you have a Homeowners Association?

Is your area flat like ours? Around here 20 acres doesn't mean privacy--we can hear the neighbors arguing 400 acres away. In the mountains 20 acres might mean you never see your neighbor's house.

Here we have sand--literally sand! --and marshy lowlands. One is bad for growing grass, the other is bad for growing sheep (hoof scald and liver fluke, anyone?). Do you understand the soil conditions and native crops in your area?

Do you have customers around? An active farmers' market? The internet?

8. Look for Your Community

We're in a rural area, but it's mostly row-crops, commercial cattle herds, and horses. Almost no sheep and very few goats. Plus, as a commercial agriculture area the use of herbicides, pesticides, antibiotics, chemical wormers, etc. is the norm. Someone with experience with sheep or alternative treatments is rare. We've had to hunt and search and scrape together a "community" to work with that understands our goals and vision for our farm operation.

Having experienced folks around to consult will save you a lot of time and money. Having access to supplies for the type of farming you want to do will make a huge difference. We still have to get a lot of our supplies by mail, although we've managed to get some of our local farm supply stores to carry a few things we use regularly. We've found that the older generations tend to have a lot of old homesteading lore stored up, they just don't think anyone needs it anymore.

The more like-minded folks in your area, the more support you'll have as you get started.

9. Check Land Uses

I run into so many people that are upset because they have to get rid of their chickens, goats, horses, you-name-it, because it turns out they're not allowed to have it in their neighborhood. And oh, the HOA rules!

Take an hour out and go up to your local Planning and Zoning or Community Development office and ask the Planners about any property you're interested in. They have plans up there spanning the next 10-30 years! They can tell you if your zoning allows livestock right now, but they can *also* tell you if that area's planned for residential in the next 20 years, or if a new road is coming through or someone wants to build a Wal-Mart nearby.

10. Think Long-Term

Everything about farming is a practice in patience. When you're thinking about investing in land, remember, you're going to be working here for *years* to make it what you want. It takes time to grow a cow, grow a garden, grow your soil.

Have you seen some of our before and after pictures? There was nothing here! Every year the grass is better...there's more fencing...the trees are taller...

You have to keep the big picture in mind!

So, what are some ideas for reducing land costs, or bringing in off-farm income to help reduce costs?

- **Rent somewhere while you build up your smaller supplies before moving to a permanent place.** You can pick up water troughs, medical supplies, hoof trimmers, buckets and scoops, feed troughs, pens, cages, nesting boxes, small chicken coops, etc. while renting and take it all with you. Maybe even tractors, mowers, trailers, etc.
- **Rent *to* another farmer until you pay down the purchasing debt.** This could be row-crops or livestock. Convert it over to your own use in small pieces as you're ready. We converted our row crop land to pasture a few acres at a time.
- **Rent-to-own.**
- **Rent your land for hunting.**
- **Timber your property.** The lumber brings in cash, and most states have replanting programs that will help defray costs of re-establishing forests. You can do a selective cut, clear-cut, or a non-commercial process with specialty harvesters.
- **Buy a small lot next to vacant land.** Rent the vacant land with an option to buy in the future.

- **Consider cost-shares and tax rebates related to establishing a conservation easement.**
- **Make sure to investigate wells and septic systems.** These can be huge costs later!
- **Rent your property for special events.** Farm and country-themed rustic weddings are all the rage right now and one good view for pictures is all it takes!
- **Rent your property for photography.** Collaborate with a local photographer to offer your property as a backdrop for their photo sessions or even a location for classes.
- **Pasture-boarding for horses.** If your fencing can contain sheep or cows, it can contain horses. If you have decent grass, you could probably find a few horse-folks with animals that would fit in just fine.
- **Work off-farm to cover your start-up costs.** Full-time farming may be more fiscally reasonable once your barns and fences are paid for and you just have to cover your operating expenses.

Finding your own place has got to be one of the hardest parts of getting started. You don't want to invest all your time and heart-blood in building a place up, developing a customer base, and then moving. But it's so hard to find something affordable if you really want to farm for a living.

****

CHAPTER THREE: BUILDINGS AND SHELTERS ON YOUR SMALL FARM OR HOMESTEAD

Buildings and Shelters--or *building shelters* as we like to do around here! --are a huge part of having livestock on a small farm or homestead. Turns out, it's also one of the more controversial topics. Infrastructure like buildings, shelters, and fencing can really add up your costs.

One of the common mantras around here for animal health is "clean and dry." Keeping your animals clean and dry is at least 80% of the health battle. Mud is a serious enemy on the natural homestead. Wet ground is the perfect home for all kinds of bacteria and parasites and being coated in mud lowers body temperatures and keeps an animal's coat from doing its normal job of warming and shedding weather.

It's important to realize that *dry* doesn't necessarily mean that the *animal* is dry-- and this is where we start to get into the controversy! We believe that God gave a cow/sheep/chicken everything they need to know to be a cow/sheep/chicken. And part of that knowledge is knowing to *come in out of the rain* if they need to. Where a lot of folks start to disagree when it comes to sheltering animals is the "if they need to" part.

We believe in doing everything we can to keep *the ground* dry and avoiding mud when possible. We use a deep bedding method to get the animals out of the mucky soup that becomes common in winter. And we believe in providing windbreaks and cover for bad precipitation. We don't believe that you should *force* the animals to use it! We don't lock animals in the barn unless we have a sick animal or a very young animal with special needs. Our shelters are all run-in environments and the animals choose whether they need to be in or not.

This drives a lot of drive-by folks *NUTS*. They believe that our animals are out in the weather because we don't provide enough shelter for them. They can't conceive of the idea that our cows are bred for hot, humid weather and *like* 90-100-degree days. They think the cows are calmly lounging in the middle of the field in July because there's not enough shade. And they can't fathom that our sheep are all wearing huge natural wool coats and *don't mind* being in the snow or light to moderate rain.

I don't say this to make you agree with me, I say it so that you know what perspective we're working from. As I mentioned in the first chapter, you always want to be sure that you're comparing apples to apples and filter opinions!

If you believe your sheep are too dumb to use the barn without help (it wouldn't surprise me if there were a few!) that's totally your call as the farmer! We certainly force enclosure for situations like hurricane predictions, etc. If you regularly get blizzards, maybe you need to consider more confinement. *You* must make this call as the farmer. But it depends on your system, your weather, and your breed of livestock—*not* what everyone else is doing!

Another concern we hear raised often is how much shelter is enough? 2-sides? 3-sides? 4-sides, fully enclosed? We believe that over-sheltering reduces your animals' overall weather-hardiness and increases dependence on sheltering. Which then increases opportunities for shelter-based health issues like pneumonia, respiratory infections from dust and mold, and physical injuries from crowding.

We believe the best option is to choose animals that are well-adapted to your location, give them as much fresh-air and sunshine as possible, and a place to get out of the mud, wind, and wet, when needed. Most of our shelters are 3-side run-in style or 2-side run-thru design. This lets the animals get in and out as needed, allows maximum air flow while preventing drafts, and blocks wind, rain, sleet, etc. These are also lighter shelters, so they are more easily portable for our rotational system.

Here's 10 questions to ask yourself before investing in any buildings or shelters.

1. What Is the Building's Purpose?

Is it going to be an animal shelter? Hay and feed storage? Tools and equipment? Will it be multi-purpose? We didn't always set out thinking multi-purpose at first, but a few years in we realized that we've re-purposed every shelter, building, lean-to, carport, and shed on our property as least once. Now we always think--how many ways can we use this in the future? Because remember—*you will change your mind*! And your operation will shift and adjust as well. Multi-purpose buildings are more cost efficient than single-purpose buildings that might end up not being needed!

2. Does It Need to Be Mobile?

We try to make everything possible mobile. That keeps the whole farmstead flexible if our needs or our interests change. What if our kiddos don't want to do chickens but we invested in a 1/4-acre permanent coop and yard? Mobile means it must be lighter and sturdier! How are you going to haul it around? By hand? By tractor? By lawn mower or 4-wheeler? It's a balance act.

We enjoy the creating, designing, and build part. There's a challenge to it that we consider an important part of our homestead journey and lifestyle. But there's also a lot of great resources out there with pre-made plans if building and inventing isn't your first love.

And here's a mistake we've made--if you're going to move it around, you have to build it so it fits through all your gates and make sure you have gates to move it around through!

3. What Else Do You Need Storage For?

This has been a serious frustration for me! Buildings and shelters on the farm are not just about the livestock. Especially if you're trying to be thrifty and save, preserve, and reuse everything! There are piles of scrap supplies; equipment, tools, and implements; feed and hay; seasonal supplies like grain feeders, hay racks, and lambing supplies...just a never-ending list of stuff you need to store.

Keeping your equipment and supplies under cover protects them and reduces deterioration and spoilage. It will lower long-term maintenance costs, but there's an upfront cost that has be balanced. And there are NEVER enough storage buildings! Something is always out in the weather that really shouldn't be.

4. Are You Sure It Should Go *There*?

If you are putting something permanent up, are you absolutely, positively, never-a-doubt-in-your-mind, dead-set that it should go *there*?

The location of our garage and the lean-to off the side of the garage were pretty much set. It was based on the location of our house and driveway. That's where they were going to be. The end.

Everything else, including gates and fence-lines, has been debated ad-nauseam and sometimes we still can't decide. And since everything is mobile, anything portable has been moved around and tried out in different locations (and usually for different purposes). And will likely be relocated again in the future. If there's any way to try a temporary solution for a year or two first, I would suggest it.

5. Are You Following Your Own Work Patterns?

This sort of follows #4...when in doubt, wait it out. Sometimes our "vision" of perfection doesn't match our real-life farm.

We've wanted to put up an equipment pole barn for years now. Cost is the reason we waited, but I'm glad we did. Why? Because by putting it off a few years, we finally saw that the building would have been on the wrong side of the farm! We kept talking about using part of the backfield right behind the garage for equipment storage, but in reality we store our equipment on "equipment row" at the back of our big field and we use the garage spot for animal handling, lambing, sick pens, and lamb harvest. Now we're talking about just putting up the shed over our existing equipment row.

If your sheep are always in the pasture, do you really need a barn by the house? Having newborns and sick animals by the house is much more important for us than having the bush hog by the house.

6. Is This Design Practical?

All farmers love big, old, musty, two-story barns. It's part of the homesteading heart! But usually they're just not practical--from the cost or design standpoint. If you're lucky enough to have one I'm sure you're finding ways to use it. But if you don't, there's probably a lot of other, more practical and economical solutions to your storage needs. On a small farm or homestead, *practical* usually means *the most use for the least money*. As everything else, this means over the long-term. Sometimes more up-front costs to get the most use, *is* the least money in the long run. And don't forget to think about maintenance when you're thinking about cost!

We use metal hut shelters the most right now. They need almost no maintenance and last a long time. We're also able to find the pieces used at auctions because they last long enough to be resold. They're big enough for our sheep, but small enough to be moved around easily with our small tractor. They keep off the wind, rain, and snow and provide shade. And they can be bedded with straw to keep the animals off the wet ground and provide warmth. The open ends mean there's no drafts, plenty of ventilation, and easy exits if someone spooks.

Our red barn was our biggest building investment other than our garage. That sturdier shelter is crucial for us to use during hurricane season. But it needs paint and a roof right now. Again.

7. Can It Be Expanded?

Most farms grow. Once you're in, you're hooked! When you're thinking about buildings and shelters, a lot of times you must think small because of your starting budget. But if you invest wisely, it will be easy to grow later.

On permanent structures, like our garage or barn, you can add lean-tos. Our garage has one on the left, and we could add one off the right or the back if we wanted too. If you put a building right up against a fence or ditch, then you've limited your expansion options.

8. Are You Reinventing the Wheel for No Reason?

To be thrifty, sometimes it's best just to copy someone that's already been there, done that.

Honestly, we don't do that very often because we enjoy the creative part. But there's nothing wrong with copying someone's success story. In his Pastured Poultry Profits book, Joel Salatin encourages folks to just copy what he did. That way you're not repeating mistakes he's already made *and corrected* for no good reason. {See RESOURCES for links.} Even if you're an inventor-creator-builder-type, I would encourage you to study what other folks have done before drawing your own design. YouTube and Google images are a great way to see other ideas before jumping into your own.

9. Do You Already Have Something You Can Use?

I formed this as a question because that's how the rest of the sections are titled. But what this should say is SAVE EVERYTHING YOU CAN.

Anything can be used on a small farm. I read about someone using an old truck camper shell as a chicken field pen. I've read about folks using pallets to make animal pens and even entire barns! We used pallets to make our garden fence to keep the dogs and sheep out. We used a dog kennel as the basis for our duck pen--which we're using today as a chicken pen.

We repurposed a cast-off greenhouse frame into a chicken hoop house. We salvaged an old pop-up camper frame to make our old chicken house mobile. Our field pen/chicken tractor is tin from an old shed someone took down and shared with us because they knew we'd use "stuff like that." We have piles of "farm junk" around because we try to keep anything that might be use-able in the future. We call it "junk" because if you're not careful it can look like a cluttered mess. But usually it's valuable supplies for future projects. This is part of being thrifty.

10. Do You Care How It Looks?

Ok, I saved this for last but it's important.

The fact is that sometimes "practical" or "frugal" can start to look junky.

Even for independent-minded self-sufficient homesteaders, this matters for a couple reasons.

- **What your husband/partner/significant other/rest-of-the-family think is important.** If they (or you!) hate rolling up in the driveway because the place looks like an abandoned farm scene from Chainsaw Massacre, well, you're going to have issues with all kinds of other stuff. Your place should bring warmth and joy and pride, and *home* to your heart--or you're not going to have the heart it takes to keep going when the going gets tough!
- **What your customers think is important.** If you want customers, you've got to consider what they think. Half your job is to educate them, and half your job is to meet their expectations. They're expecting something from Old McDonald's or Mother Goose. You probably can't give them *that*, but you can meet them in the middle. If all your offering is Chainsaw Massacre, they probably won't be back.
- **What the public thinks is important.** It's an unpleasant fact, but when it comes to farm animals, most people are ignorant *and* judgmental. If folks *think* your place looks like crap, they are going to *think* your animals are

treated like crap. And they're going to call *someone* and complain. You're going to have a big headache. More people I know have gotten rid of their livestock because of neighbor complaints than because of financial issues. Most are completely unfounded and due to simple ignorance, but there it is. Most are not *forced* to get rid of their animals, they just get tired of feeling harassed.

Here's the thing, *you, as the farmer, need to know what you're about*. You need to know what your animals need and what they don't. You need to know what you're doing and why-or why not. You need to keep all these things in mind, think carefully, and make the best decisions for your place--and be ready to stand by them. It's just part of farming in today's world.

****

CHAPTER FOUR: FOOD AND WATER ON YOUR SMALL FARM OR HOMESTEAD

By far the biggest small farm or homestead budget line item (other than a mortgage) is the feed bill. Food and water are the bottom line in your small farm enterprise. If you don't have them, everything else needs to go!

Here are some thoughts to evaluate your own options moving forward.

- **Junk in, junk out.** You are what you eat. This is even more true for your animals. What you feed is key to what you produce.
- **Consistency is key.** Animals don't adjust easily to feed changes, whether composition, amount, or even timing. A consistent feed product and consistent feeding routine will eliminate a lot of health concerns before they even get started. You need to establish dependable supplies.
- **It's easier to match your animals to the available feed than to match feed to the animals.** Find livestock breeds/individuals that can thrive with your existing farm conditions. If you're going to feed grass, have good grazers!

So naturally, the place to start would be at the bottom.

Grass

Assuming you have grass on your farm, this is one time where cheap and easy really does equal healthier!

If you're in a situation like we were when we started and you don't have any grass—it's an uphill battle and the feed bills are large. But we're committed to a grass-based system and every year we have a bit *more* grass, and feed *less* hay, and the ledger balances better accordingly.

You can get a great health breakdown on a grass-based approach in Jo Robinson's book Pasture Perfect. It's a quick and easy read from a journalist who uncovered an amazing amount of research on the benefits of eating grass-fed food. {See RESOURCES for links.}

When it comes to the benefits of a grass-based system for your farm and livestock, most books these days start on the premise that you already know grass-fed is best. If you're on the fence about how important a grass-based system is for the small farm, I would suggest starting with All Flesh is Grass by Gene Logsdon. {See RESOURCES for links.} He goes over the whole, big picture. Once you're convinced that grass is the key, then I would strongly suggest Small Scale Livestock Farming by Carol Ekarius. {See RESOURCES for links.} It is an excellent overview laying out a diversified, grass-based livestock plan. It will give you all the basics to understand rotational grazing, multi-species grazing, and high-level farm planning.

Managing grass is an art form. It takes a lot of research, study, and trial and error. But here's something to keep in mind about grass and rotational grazing-- you don't need troughs, buckets, pans. You don't need to scrub anything. You don't need a tractor to move it. You don't need a trailer to haul it. You don't need any muscles to unload it. And once it's there, it doesn't cost anything for the animals to harvest it. The cost benefits for a small farm are infinite.

Hay

Ok, but even in the best circumstances there are seasons without grass, right?

Not necessarily!

Hay is grass that was cut while fresh, dried, and then baled and stored for later in the season. Much like the difference between fresh and dried fruit, it loses nutritional quality from the fresh source but the better it was to begin with, the better it is dehydrated.

Hay as a feed source is much trickier to manage than it seems at first. There's more to it than just buying a bale and tossing it out there. Sometimes we've found a great hay source, but they run out before the season is over and we have to switch producers. Not ideal.

Sometimes we find a consistent source, but the nutritional quality is low, and we have to supplement to maintain body condition. Not ideal.

Or you find a great source but can't afford it. Or you find a great source, but you don't have somewhere to store it all winter, so you start losing bales to mold and mildew.

Then there's the idea of baling it yourself. That's a great idea! But it takes a lot of equipment, storage and supplies. You need a consistent nutritional value and the same combination of art and science that goes into growing good grass goes into making good hay. Knowing when to cut, when to bale, how to store…It's just not as easy as it first seems. We've had our fields custom-baled, but in the early years we found that the nutritional quality wasn't there yet, and it was better for the animals' health if we bought high-quality hay from an experienced producer.

We feed free choice hay all winter from around the end of November when the grass starts to die off to around March when fresh grass comes back. We prefer to only grain our ewes in late pregnancy, if possible. We found that there's a cost-benefit break point with cheap hay. With poor quality hay, we have to supplement more to make up the nutritional difference so what we save on hay we're spending on grain. It's a poor trade for your animals and your pocketbook!

You also have to determine your feeding methods. We have constructed several different feeders over the years from pallets and hog panels. Small ones to go around standard round bales. A big one to go with large square bales. A top-fill option to use with small square bales. And we have one rack/trough combo unit that we use in our lambing fields. It's all trial and error, so borrow or buy used to start with and figure out what you like.

Grain

Again, in a grass-based system, grain is a supplement, and amounts will be determined by the nutritional quality of your forage. The key is to have a consistent mixture and feed with routine amounts and times. We've tried everything from supplementing only with corn, to mixing our own feed, to bagged feeds.

We live in an area that's not known for sheep, so mixing our own feed was challenging. We couldn't find the grains or additions we wanted without special ordering, which was dangerous unless you ordered the entire winter upfront. Who knows when a shipment would be delayed or cancelled? Plus, all the shipping costs!

Supplementing with only corn during lambing works for several other sheep producers we know. But in consultation with our vet over the first couple years that wasn't a good option for us because our hay was just not a consistently high quality. Our animals needed more than just calories from the corn. Remember that apples to apples conversation? We couldn't copy a system from a "good grass" area because we didn't have "good grass."

So, we started getting some of our hay tested and went to a general-ration bagged feed as a grain supplement with free choice hay the second half of the winter when our ewes were in late pregnancy and early nursing. We saw a significant improvement in body condition, so this is a program we've stuck with. We still experienced some supply challenges at first because the local feed stores were not carrying enough sheep feed consistently for our operation over the winter. One feed store even told us we were the only one buying it. This is where that note in Chapter 2 comes from—know what community you're moving into. We are not in a sheep community.

Eventually we went to buying an entire pallet of feed from Tractor Supply Company at the beginning of the season so we don't have to worry about them running out when we need it. That also gave us a bulk discount *and* the option of using a coupon! There are a lot of ways to secure your winter feed supply, but we have found for the animals health and welfare (which is good for your bank account as well!) it's best to lay in your winter feed supply at the beginning of the season.

We use a plain old, open trough feed bunk for the cows. Works great. The sheep are a little trickier because they are crazy about food! The pregnant ewes will leap up in that wide trough and slip and slid and even flip over trying to get to the feed first. We had to make them wooden feeders that are too narrow for them to jump in. This is another way that you do what works for your operation and not just go with what the store or other farmers are doing.

Water

Water supply is a big deal here in Virginia where the summers can easily spend weeks in the 100-degree range. We have the water, but we've got to be able to get it out to the animals.

Our super-duper, fancy "system" for watering?

Hoses. We just use garden hoses.

And when the hoses are frozen, we use 5-gallon buckets.

We started with cheap green ones that only last a few seasons, and slowly replaced those via clearance sales with commercial ones. They run all over the farm along the fence lines so they don't get mowed. Most of the time. We use black rubber 40-gallon troughs that can be dumped and moved with the animals from pasture to pasture. They're very easy to clean.

We have one large galvanized one that we will use in the summer as a backup water source in really hot weather. The cows can drink up a lot more water than the sheep!

As discussed in Chapter 3, we have held off on installing permanent water lines for cost reasons *and* design reasons. The hose system lets us determine what lines and layout we really need before we invest in trenching across the farm.

****

CHAPTER FIVE: HEALTH AND WELLNESS ON YOUR SMALL FARM OR HOMESTEAD

I think this topic gets to the core of the hard part of livestock farming. The opposite side of *health and wellness* is *sickness and death*. They are two sides of the same coin and they are both found on the small farm. *And it can be hard!* And expensive.

Expensive in dollars and cents *and* in heartache and misery. The good news is that as a small farmer you have a lot of control over this. Not total control--that's up to the good Lord! --but you do have a lot of influence over outcomes. The biggest factor in our animals' health and wellness has been *our* experience as farmers. The better we've gotten at taking care of them, the more they have thrived. But gaining that experience was sometimes very expensive.

Here's a simple 4-step process we've tried to use to control health expenses on our small farm.

1. **Create a healthy environment**
2. **Match your animals to that environment**
3. **Create a healthy routine of care**
4. **Provide for expert help when needed**

Easy to say, harder to execute. The definition of what constitutes "healthy" will depend on what system you use on your farm. Different farm philosophies will accept different levels of health, welfare, and loss. If you want to be organic, only use herbal health products, or be 100% grass-fed, you may have a different standard for healthcare, acceptable medications, and humane practices than a commercial operation.

Here are some basic thoughts on each area for you to consider.

1. Create a Healthy Environment

Here's a common oversimplification--*healthy animals cost less than sick animals*.

This is a dangerous ground for a new farmer or homesteader. Why? Because healthy animals don't happen by luck or magic. They happen because the farmer *invests* in their health and well-being--and that's usually not cheap!

For example: A farmer says he has hay for $60 a round bale. Ouch. But you talk to him and he says, *Well, what'cha feeding? Sheep and cows? I got some cow hay out back for $30 a bale.* Hmmm...

In our experience "cow hay" is hay that is either old and moldy, stored outside and moldy, baled badly and moldy...Seeing the common denominator here? The thought is that cows are less sensitive to mold and mildew than, say, horses, so you can feed them "junk" hay and they won't get sick and you just make up the nutritional difference with grain. But a grass-based operation doesn't want to make up the difference in grain! And remember, *junk in-junk out*. The extra cost is an investment in the animals' health and welfare upfront to (hopefully) avoid expensive veterinary care later.

Simple keys for a healthy environment

- Clean and dry shelters and bedding
- Quality feed and clean, fresh water
- Low stress lifestyle
- Quarantine all new animals

The idea is to reduce the risks of your animals being exposed to parasites and bacteria that could make them sick, while leaving them strong enough to naturally fight off anything they are exposed to.

2. Match Your Animals to Your Environment

The more you can use your farm environment without modification, the less expensive your enterprise will be. Our Zebu cows like the heat, so we don't have to invest in as many barns, shades, and fans. Certain breeds of sheep do well in hot climates and don't have to be sheared—shearing can be expensive! Some breeds of laying chickens are better cold-weather layers than others. I'll cover this more in Chapter 6, but the idea is that the more your animals are adapted to your environment the less you'll have to provide (and pay for) as the farmer.

3. Create a Routine for Preventative Health Care

This one is going to be based on your specific values and vision for your farm, but everyone that has animals on the homestead should have a basic healthcare plan.

I know of several traditional commercial sheep operations that de-worm their animals every 4-6 weeks. I know of at least two "alternative treatment" farms which never use commercial chemical de-wormers on their sheep, and use a routine of pasture rotation, vinegar and garlic in the drinking water, and herbal de-wormers every couple of months to maintain the health of their flock.

Both have pros and cons, risks and costs, and the point here is not which is better. The point is that one relies on mostly direct treatment inputs and one relies on a mix of direct treatments and environmental adjustments for preventative care.

To understand the cost for your small farm, you must determine which path you're going to take and research the costs of your inputs. Then to keep costs as low as possible for your choice, you need to develop a systematic approach to implementing it so you're not over or under-treating at any time. Worming is one example, but vaccines, hoof trims, shearing, and tail docking are all health care actions that should be conscientiously considered, scheduled, and routinely managed in the life of a livestock farmer.

Preventative care is also where I would put the hard decisions of whom to cull. Some animals are naturally more resistant to sickness or parasites. You want to build up your home flock with these strong and resistant animals and weed out the ones that are always sickly or struggling.

This doesn't have to mean harvesting the animal for food. Sometimes that animal is just not a good fit for your environment or management system. Sometimes you'll have an ewe that just doesn't do well with the pushing and shoving at the feed trough and is being constantly out-competed and underfed in the winter. But she might be just fine as a field companion for a lonely horse or in a smaller backyard hobby flock. Everyone (including your wallet!) will be happier with her culled from your flock and moved somewhere else.

4. Provide for Expert Help When Needed

Notice I didn't say *call the vet*. Depending on your problem and your level of experience, your neighbor might be the only help you need. The point is to create a network of knowledge that you can tap into. I've gotten help from other farmers, from books, from Facebook groups, from equipment suppliers, and yes, from our local large-animal vet. Some options cost more than others. The key is to build relationships so you can *get help when you need it*--because in a health emergency, timing it critical to success.

Expert help was expensive for us in the beginning because we simply didn't know anyone else locally that knew anything about sheep. Pretty much our only hands-on resource was our vet. *Cha-ching!* Our vet bills were neck and neck with our feed bills the first year or two!

Is it coincidence that our vet care expenses when down when our feed bill went up? Eh, maybe not. Once we found a steady supply of high-quality hay, had quality grass coming up, and hit a grain-supplementing routine that worked, our farm visits dropped to practically zero. Our preventative health care routines were definitely working! Plus, we had developed a relationship with our vet, so they felt comfortable giving some phone consultation if we had something crop up, and that was free.

An unpleasant by-product of becoming a more experienced livestock farmer is facing the decision that an animal situation is not worth calling the vet for.

Ouch. I *hate* this part.

When you can call the vet, sometimes it just means you have someone backing up your decision to give up. *A professional who agrees with you*. When you make that call yourself, it's much more painful.

However, making that call is not just a straight cost-benefit ratio like you might think. Even in cases where we know the animal will never be profitable again, we may still call the vet if it's highly likely they can save the animal's life. Not all commercial operations would make this choice, but it's part of who we are.

We'll also call, even on a lost cause, if we think there is something significant, we can learn from them being out here for us to know next time for ourselves.

Something we've never seen before. Something we want to understand to try and prevent in the future. We use those vet calls as expensive but irreplaceable learning opportunities to make us better farmers. Take time to get as much out of every vet visit as you can!

You'll notice that I didn't really get into any recommendations on what you should decide to do. This workbook is meant to be a decision-making tool, not recommendations. These are all things to think through as you're making your plans and getting started. You'll find a helpful decision-making matrix in the WORKSHEET section, but it's *your* decisions that will shape what *your* farm or homestead looks like!

****

CHAPTER SIX: CHOOSING LIVESTOCK FOR YOUR SMALL FARM OR HOMESTEAD

Now we get to the fun part of a small livestock farm--the critters!

It's the part we tend to get over-zealous and the most impulsive about. And probably the part where it's most important that we take our time and think things through!

On a serious note, as described in the INTRODUCTION, it really is the part people most often get in over their head with. We've ended up with a lot of cast-off livestock over the years. From adopting chickens at the animal shelter, to a goat tied to our porch rail, to a horse it took us almost 3 years to re-home properly...stray dogs, stray cats, miniature goats that failed as pasture companions, and even peacocks. We've taken in so many animals from people who weren't thinking long-term about their animals and see all our grass and think that's all you need to make it work.

And we usually always say yes, because let's be honest, all small farmers are animal lovers at heart. You have to be to do this job.

When it comes to bringing livestock onto the farm, there's several broad areas you need to think through.

- **Are you ready for livestock on your farm or homestead?**
- **What type of livestock should you have on your farm or homestead?**
- **What specific breed of livestock should you have on your farm or homestead?**

Here's some serious thoughts about how to choose the right livestock for your small farm.

Are You Ready for Livestock on Your Farm?

It seems like a natural progression. You buy property, put up a fence, add some sheep, and you've got a regular Green Acres going on.

But let's look a little deeper at our preparations here, and some of the specific ways folks go wrong.

- **Are you *allowed* to have animals on your property?** Farms and homesteads come in all shapes and sizes, but as I mentioned in Chapter 1, you really need to check with your local planning, zoning, or community development office about your property. A lot of folks have ended up with a violation notice for having backyard chickens in zoning districts which don't allow livestock.

- **Are your animals going to be pets, or food?** I'd take my free Craigslist dog to the vet no matter what. He's a pet. He's family. We won't take a $10 chicken to the vet unless we think it's something contagious. To gauge the resources you need, you need to understand your personal boundaries when it comes to the animals on your farm. The Health and Wellness Chapter addresses this deeper.

- **Do you have space for animals?** Are you familiar with the concept of stocking rates and carrying capacity? A great primer here would be Small Scale Livestock Farming by Carol Ekaruis. She covers almost all these questions in a few paragraphs and pages. {See RESOURCES for links.}

- **Do you have the infrastructure for animals you want?** You'll need more than just a fence. You'll need shelters, equipment storage, feeders, waterers, feed storage, medicine, and medicine storage. The list goes on. Even what type of fencing you need is driven by what animals you want to have.

- **Do you have the equipment for the animals you want?** Everyone has a different opinion of what that means. I'd say every livestock farmer should at least have a truck and trailer, but I've seen people transport cows in the back of their station wagon, so I'm not going to go too far into this. *The best bet is to just assess what you think you'll need and whether you have access to it when you need it.* If your animals come once and leave once, maybe you just hire someone to transport. If you know you're moving animals to market once or twice a year, every year, maybe you need your own trailer. And how many animals? What size animals? We hauled up to 10 sheep in an 8 ft truck bed with a camper shell on top. We didn't get a full-sized trailer until we also had cows and horses.

- **Will you process your own animals?** That comes with a completely different set of supplies. And if you don't think you will to begin with, then you need to think about transportation equipment to get your animals to the processor--and whether one is nearby or not!

- **Are you taking a natural/holistic health approach, conventional health approach, or a mixed approach?** Again, I addressed this in depth in the Health and Wellness Chapter, but it deserves repeating because when you bring animals home you'll need to make immediate decisions on quarantine processes, integration with existing animals, and how to use a systematic approach to whole-farm health. Having learned the hard way, we quarantine all outside animals in our "sick pen" or "sacrifice pasture" for a week while we administer wormer, trim hooves, treat hooves with Hoof-n-Heel multiple times, and introduce them to our food routine.

- **Are you using a grass-based, rotational model, or grain-based, fixed-pasture model?** You're going to want to choose breeds that thrive within your management style and environment or you're going to spend a lot of extra resources creating accommodations for them. A commercial feedlot animal is not going to thrive if you throw them out on pasture. A tropical, hair sheep breed is not going to thrive in New England winters.

- **Do you have the financial resources to be a responsible owner?** There will be vet bills, fencing repair bills, feed bills, costs for minerals, salt, wormer, vaccines, syringes, hoof trimmers, buckets. So. Many. Buckets. I, personally don't believe that raising your own meat is always more frugal that the grocery store, but even if it was, you still have to upfront all the costs and only see the savings on the backend of the budget. Something to keep in mind.

- **Do you have any experience with livestock?** *This is not a make or break question.* I didn't. I took horseback riding lessons and owned a dog. And that was the extent of my hands-on ownership experience before we brought our first sheep home. You'll learn. It's just good to be honest about your current situation and be ready to ask for help. Have your experts lined up!

These are all very technical details about livestock ownership, but let's also hit on some of the "heart issues" if you will. The emotional issues. The ones that really seem to be the make or break when it comes to the farm life. And I'd like to offer some truth *and* some encouragement here. I didn't have any hands-on experience for 90% of the things that are listed below. I don't think you have to know the answers to all of these. You just need to honestly run them through your mind and give them serious consideration. Not, *oh yeah, I'll be fine with that, I've watched homesteading shows on the Discovery channel* --I mean real consideration.

1. **Are you ready for the dirt, smell, and chaos?** This is not just about animal smells in the barnyard. Oh no. There are seasons when our whole house smells like wet wool and cow mud. Not the farm, the HOUSE. Why? Because we're so busy outside that we're running back and forth, mucking up the floors, and throwing dirty farm clothes in the mudroom that I don't have time to wash! I don't know any farmer that hasn't eventually had to bring a young or sick animal in the house. Are you ready to physically tackle and wrestle a calf with scours (that's really icky diarrhea, in case you didn't know) to give them meds and clean them up? If you are a Type A, Clorox-cleaning home-keeper, you really need to think about this one. Especially if you are going to pull your children fully into the farm life with you. There. will. be. mess. Your routines will be off. Kids will miss bedtime and sometimes even homework because something so amazing and in-the-moment-REAL is happening that we don't want them to want to miss it. *During certain seasons or emergencies, you just have to give yourself grace. The farm life is not like everyone else's everyday life.*

2. **Are you ready to be a doctor?** In the Health and Wellness Chapter, I talk about having a relationship with your vet and that expertise can't be replaced. But as a livestock farmer, you are going to have to learn so much hands-on, basic medical care. Partly because of the expense of calling the vet, and partly because your animal can't always wait. Are you ready to be bloody from tending emergency wounds, or covered in birth fluid from helping with lambing? Are you ok with having sheep burp up grass cud and baking soda on you? Are you squeamish about sticking an animal with a needle or scraping manure and rot out of hooves? These are basic care issues on the farm. You, the farmer, will do the worming, trim hooves, give vaccines, clean and disinfect flesh wounds. You'll have to do all the after care and follow-up care when the vet leaves from an emergency illness. I've given antibiotic shots, administered fluids, flushed abscess, stomach-tubed lambs...the list goes on. *If you're not ready, that's ok. You just need to know it's coming and you're up for the challenge.*

- **Are you ready for death?** This is the hardest part of livestock farming no matter what circumstances surround it. Animals die, and a lot of times you have no idea why. We've had the vet come out and say, *we have no idea but there's nothing else we can do.* We've nursed animals' night and day and still lost them. We've had predators break into the chicken coop and kill half the flock in one night! The other half of the question is even harder.

- **Are you ready for killing? Are you ready to have to put an animal down? Are you ready to shoot a predator to defend your livestock? Are you ready to harvest animals that you grew for food?** These are tough questions and I see so many new homesteaders asking when it gets easier or how do you get over it. *You never get over it.* It doesn't get easier. You just learn to accept it and to handle it as quickly and humanely as possible. And when you do that, you'll find an amazing peace in the natural flow of life on the farm.

- **Are you ready to be scrutinized, criticized, and harassed?** This is unfortunate but real. Animals attract people like a moth to a flame, and people are ignorant. Bless their hearts. I talked about this a lot more in the Buildings and Shelters Chapter, but be prepared for *everyone* to have an opinion on what you're doing. Also be prepared for people to do stupid things like *moooo* at your cows as they drive by, chase your chickens when they come to visit, and wander too close to the electric fence just to see if the warning sign is *for real*. Be sure you're comfortable with setting rules, educating guests, and knowing what your liability coverage is.

- **Are you ready to hate it?** Look, it happens. You get a handful of chickens just for your own eggs, and it turns out you're getting 4-5 eggs a day, which is more than 2 dozen eggs a week, which is way more than you, your neighbor, your pastor, and your parents can eat--not to mention everyone else local also has a couple chickens in *their* backyard for *their* own eggs. So now you're hip deep in eggs and your family threatens to revolt if you serve one more quiche. Do you have an exit strategy? *It might just one enterprise, or it might be the whole farming-homesteading lifestyle, there's no reason to spend so much time, energy, money, and heartache doing something you detest day in and day out.*

Life on a small farm is hard, even on good days. Running through these questions can help you make better choices as you get started and not set yourself up for failure.

What Type of Livestock Should You Have on Your Farm?

Choosing the right animals to fit your needs, your goals, and your farm space will make the best use of your limited resources and be less stressful for you AND the animals.

If your tractor dies, there will be financial pain and angst. When you lose a mature, well-producing ewe that you've raised from birth, carried through 5 pregnancies, and recently sat up through the night giving fluids, antibiotics, and watching her fade away...well, there's costs and then there's costs.

One thing about small farms is you often hear people talk about not getting attached because you know you're going to harvest the animal. *That's not completely true!* If you have layers, you're not harvesting the hens, you're harvesting the eggs, so you can be attached to them! They're going to be around for a while. In our breeding flock of sheep, the lambs are born in February and sold in September/October. But the ewes and ram stay for years. You can get attached to them! You can name them! You can *know* them. That's the fun part of livestock farming. You want to be sure you have animals on the farm that you *enjoy* being around--because you're going to be around them a lot.

The first thing when considering what type of livestock to raise is **SMALLER = LESS**.

A chicken costs less than a sheep. A sheep cost less than a cow. A chicken coop cost less than a barn. Constructing a sheep pen takes less material than constructing a cattle pen. Chickens will fit in the backseat of a car, sheep will fit in the back of a truck, a full-grown cow is usually going to require a trailer. Chickens eat less than sheep, sheep eat less than cows, everything eats less than horses. {smile} So size really does matter.

The only place this really breaks down is in labor.

Labor investment is really about your management style, not the size of the animals. For example, a rotational grazing system, where the animals are basically feeding themselves 70% of the time can be light on manual labor for most of the year. However, a stationary chicken house requires a lot of cleaning, bedding, changing, disinfecting and maintenance.

Another example is that a multi-species grazing system means that your sheep, cows, and even chickens are all eating the same thing at the same time and sharing a water source--less labor. Keeping species separate (which we do for different seasons) increases your workload because you must provide shelter, food, and water to each location.

Here are some questions to consider when deciding what type of livestock will suit your farm.

How much experience do you have?

Be honest. We're talking hands-on experience here, not book learning. Like I've said before, I had basically *none*. All animals can be dangerous and unpredictable. Being flogged by a rooster is no joke. But I'll take an angry rooster over an angry bull any day! Less experience means smaller animals are probably a better way *to start*. I'm not trying to wreak any dreams here; I'm just staying *to start with*! Sheep were our goal when we started out, but the first livestock on our farm were bantam chickens. Then sheep. Then full-sized chickens. Then cows, then a donkey, then horses.

This gets to the male/female question as well. Personal anecdotes to the side, uncastrated male animals are more challenging to handle than female animals. No matter what species, if you're a newbie and it's bigger than a chicken I would strongly suggest no males for the first year or two. Usually, you can start with already-bred animals or borrow a breeding male once a year for a fee until you get your feet under you in the handling department.

How knowledgeable are you?

Here's where I'm taking books, as well as real life experience. Every species has different food, shelter, and healthcare needs. Some are similar and some are not. Sheep and goats are very similar. Sheep and chickens, not so much.

So how much do you know about the animals that you want? Do you know food/shelter/breeding differences between chickens and ducks? Do you know the copper toxicity differences between sheep and cows? Do you know the foraging differences between donkeys and horses?

There's a danger in thinking that a similar size, shape, or diet automatically make animals work well together in the big picture. For example, rotating sheep and cows on the same pasture can break parasite cycles because they are affected by different bugs. Rotating sheep and goats won't because they share the same parasites. Sheep and goats will re-infect each other. And don't even get me started on the differences between egg layers and meat broilers! This is where book research can help you develop a good overall plan. I'd recommend Barnyard in Your Backyard and The Backyard Homestead Guide to Raising Farm Animals as good overviews of all the different livestock types and needs. . {See RESOURCES for links.}

Sometimes it's best to take things one species at a time and get the hang of that species before adding anything new.

What do you eat? What products do you need?

This gets back to knowing what your farm is all about. Are you a homesteader raising your own food? Well, if you don't eat alpaca, then don't raise it. If it's important to you that you process your own food, then how comfortable are you with that part of the job? If you're new, maybe start with chickens or rabbits-- probably the easiest home-processing. If you've done deer before, you're probably fine with a sheep or goat. Hogs and cows take more know how--as well as more equipment and space!

Are you looking for milk to drink or milk for soap? Or both?! Have you tasted the difference between raw, home-pasteurized, and commercial-pasteurized milk? Raw milk is an acquired taste.

Do you want to make your own socks and sweaters? Cows, chickens, and goats won't help with that.

Do you know what type of animal produces what you want? The number of people who asked us if we ate veal when we started raising sheep was *astounding*! Do you want laying hens or meat broilers? You *can* eat a layer, but good luck getting eggs from a Cornish-Cross! And if you just want eggs, you don't really need a rooster.

What will you sell?

If you're just trying to be self-sufficient, the question is just what you eat. But if you're looking to make a profit, then you need to have a product to sell. You need to think about what market you have access to. Is meat your main product or are you looking for a value-added or cottage industry product?

The market for raw wool is practically non-existent if you want a profit. Cleaned fleeces are a little bit better because hand-spinning is popular at the moment. But the average crafter doesn't know what to do with wool until it's yarn. Yarn also ships easier than a whole fleece. Do you know how to get from the back of a sheep to a skein of yarn?

And do you want multi-purpose species? (Also known as dual purpose, although it's sometimes more than two.) Wool sheep can be for meat, wool, lambskin, and milk. Hair sheep are a meat and hide animals only. Cows can be for meat or milk, or in rare cases cow hide, broiler chickens are only going to be for meat. Llamas? I have no idea.

Who will you sell to?

Meat rabbits come to mind for me here. I don't know anyone that eats rabbit except people that hunt their own rabbit. I, personally, don't know who that market it. Make sure to do your market research.

Our lamb market is an ethnic market so they are very familiar with the product and prefer to self-process their lambs. For our market, we don't have to worry about USDA labeling, etc. We sell live animals to the buyer and they arrange their own processing. But we know other breeders that mostly sell to restaurants and had to find a processor, get a label, and other selling steps.

Joel Salatin's book You Can Farm talks about choosing ventures, stacking enterprises, and making a profit in detail. His book Family Friendly Farming also addresses both profitability and holistic farm decision-making. And they're very encouraging and positive. If making money on your farm is important to your goals, I would definitely read through these two early on. He also talks about strategies to successfully introduce customers to new products to sell what *you* want to sell. Small Scale Livestock Farming is also a great introductory resource for profitability. {See RESOURCES for links.}

What Specific Breed of Livestock Should You Have on Your Farm?

You've already decided that you're ready to bring some livestock out to the farm. You've done your research and planning and know what type of livestock you want to start with. But within each species there is a huge list of individual breeds to choose from. And each one has plenty of breeders and admirers swearing that theirs is the *best breed ever*!

The Livestock Conservancy identifies and tracks heritage livestock breeds *only*, and they have lists of 22 breeds of cattle, 10 individual breeds of hogs, 12 different rabbits, 22 breeds of sheep, and so many poultry it's a completely different list! How do you choose one?

You need to take an honest look at 3 things on the farm, then do some breed-specific research, and match your breed research to your farm.

1. **Your Farm Goals**
2. **Your Farm Environment**
3. **Your Farm System**

Here's the thing that you really need to know--*there are pros and cons to every breed.* It's unlikely that any animal is going to fit in your system perfectly. You'll have to weigh the good and the bad to find what you can live with.

YOUR Farm Goals

I can't stress enough to know *your* purpose. This is critical when it comes to breed selection. If your goal is to make a profit, you need to be able to buy low enough and sell high enough to make a consistent profit and have a sustainable market. It takes a lot of lamb chops to pay for an $800 ram and two $600 ewes, plus feed for a year, before you see your first product.

Is your goal food production, a cottage industry, or just self-sufficiency? If your goal is handmade wool socks and dryer balls, then hair sheep breeds are a *bad* choice. If you want to make wool *clothing* like sweaters, scarves, or hats, then you need to focus on a high-quality wool producer. Our Clun Forest sheep are considered dual purpose, but their wool is more suited for rugs and outerwear. A true fiber artist is probably going to be looking for something finer.

Do you have any important farm values or philosophies to consider? Perhaps you want to focus strictly on American breeds. Or only critically endangered breeds. Or only breeds native to your area.

Or none of these? Maybe the driving force of your farm is training herding dogs. I know several farmers that got into raising geese or sheep because they were training their dogs.

Let those values guide a lot of your research. That will give you a stronger sense of purpose and fulfillment on the tough days, or even tough years. That sense of purpose will help you make the call when it comes to quantity vs quality. And it will help you find a community or network of other farmers with common goals to work with.

YOUR Farm Environment

We live in Coastal Virginia. We have hot, humid, and sometimes very dry summers. We have unpredictable, but usually mild and mediocre, winters. In the spring and fall, we have good rainfall, lots of mosquitos, and hurricane season. Our Zebu cattle are originally an African breed and do well in our summers. They dislike snow, so our mild winters work for them too. They have a decent natural parasite resistance which is a big help here where the moisture and humidity mean we have high parasite-loading.

What is your environment like? There's no need to spend all your resources fighting your livestock's natural characteristics when you could choose wisely and have them work *for you* rather than against you. Do you get a lot of snow? Our Zebu would be miserable, and I would need a much bigger barn! Of course, shaggy Highlands would do well, and be miserable *here* in the summer.

YOUR Farm System

This is probably the most important factor. When researching breeds, you need to go beyond the websites and books and talk to the people raising them. And you need to talk to people raising them *the way you are going to raise them!* That apples-to-apples farm system comparison I was talking about earlier in this book.

Urban or backyard chickens are a big thing right now. It's important to realize that a lot of articles about chicken healthcare are written from that perspective and a "pastured poultry for-profit" model will have little in common with that. Similarly, our mobile hoop house model has little in common with a fully-enclosed backyard coop. My chickens are exposed to different dangers, different parasites, different weather conditions.

Are you planning on being organic? You need to look for hearty breeds because your wellness options can be limited. Will your animals be grazing far from your home place or not under constant supervision? You probably want a breed with a strong natural flocking characteristic as a protective measure.

Here are a few other questions to ask yourself.

- **Can I find these animals around me?** Will I have to travel a lot to bring original and/or replacement stock to the farm? (That can be a big cost!)

- **Do I plan on selling breeding stock?** Will anyone else want to buy this breed from me? Do registrations and bloodlines matter? These are all additional expenses, but we have found that selling one breeding lamb pays for the total upfront cost of the ewe-whereas it takes almost 3 meat lambs to cover the purchase cost of the ewe.

- **Is there enough genetic diversity available to me in this breed for me to find healthy replacement stock or new bloodlines?** This can be a big deal with rare and endangered heritage breeds! If you're required to import semen for artificial insemination (AI) from the UK, well, your budget needs to reflect that!

- **Do my targeted customers have a preference I should consider?** We have customers that find tail-docking offensive and we find it to be a required management practice in our humid area. If they were our only customers, perhaps we would want to consider a fat-tailed sheep that doesn't need to be docked.

- **Will I be breeding my own replacement stock?** Do I have facilities for that? Or will I be buying replacement animals? This will affect your seasonal cash flow. We breed our own replacement ewes, but usually buy an outside ram for genetic diversity. We buy all our chickens and don't even keep a rooster around (most of the time).

- **Do looks matter?** You'll have to see these animals every. single. day. Pick something you like the looks of, not just something you think will make money. I enjoy looking at our ewe's faces. They have a clean, bright-eyed, intelligent look to them. It makes the pasture work more enjoyable. With our chickens, we like a diversity of colors and a full-bodied, even over-fluffed look. Some of our Reds tend to be scrawny and "efficient" looking. That's just their body type, but I'm always a little worried about them. You don't need any more worry in your days!

- **Does intelligence matter?** There's dumb, and then there's dumb. We have some chickens that run for cover when they see a shadow overhead and some that just stand there staring up at it. If you're free ranging, this kind of stuff matters. If your coop is fully enclosed, not so much. You also need to think about traits like skittishness and aggressiveness. Both are a headache.

There's always crossbreds and mixed breeds and unidentified "barnyard" breeds too. We have some Hog Island/Clun Forest crossbreds on the farm and they are excellent ewes!

Or you can throw all this to the wind and come home with whatever you saw at the farm auction or show too. We've all done *that* at least once! But it always works out best in the long run if you sit down and think about it first. Especially when it comes to making good financial decisions on the farm. And the animals will certainly appreciate it!

****

CHAPTER SEVEN: YOUR SMALL FARM OR HOMESTEAD GARAGE

At this point we've discussed a lot of about the dollars and cents of starting a small farm from the livestock side. If you're raising animals, that's where a lot of your costs come from! But sometimes we skip over the construction and mechanical side of things. The *fix-it* side of things is important when discussing dollars and cents because *doing your own construction and maintenance work is a huge factor in controlling your costs*! Labor for mechanical work usually runs at 50% of the total price—so doing your own repairs just saved you an automatic 50%!

First, your small farm or homestead is going to have what I would consider regular maintenance and repairs. Regular maintenance is the little routine things like changing your fluids and tires, painting your buildings, tightening fences and replacing latches or knobs.

Then there's what I would call heavy-maintenance and farm construction. It doesn't have to be done often, but it is eventually required just from normal wear and tear. Working on bigger things like alternators, water pumps, carburetors, and building projects like barns, coops, new fences, or shade shelters.

The more you're able to do yourself the more you're going to save on the cost of doing business.

What Do You Need to Have?

Someone on a homesteading forum recently asked, *what are your essential tools if you were starting a homestead?* I think the question is a little overwhelming! It's also extremely dependent on your personal skill set as well as the size and nature of your individual homestead. Remember, the best tools to have are ones you know how to use! Around here we tackle just about everything from oil changes to barn construction ourselves, so our "essential" tool list reflects that.

What you *need* is the tools for the jobs you do!

Here are some categories you could break it down into to start getting a grasp on it.

- **Gardening and growing tools.** Rakes, shovels, hoes, buckets, hoses, sprinklers, pruners, weed trimmer, mower, rototiller, chain saw, etc.
- **Infrastructure building and maintenance tools.** Fence supplies, hammers, screwdrivers, pliers, saw, sander, grinder, paint supplies, nuts and bolts, nails and screws, sawhorses.
- **Mechanic tools.** The stuff you need for working on all your other stuff! Wrenches, sockets and drivers, oil filter wrenches and oil pans, crowbars, jack and jack stands, air compressor and air tools.

Where Do You Get What You Need?

Our garage is a conglomeration of tools that we each had before getting married, and what we've acquired slowly over the last 20 years. We inherited some things, like our air compressor. We've also had a lot passed to us from family members that were moving, retiring, or downsizing their hobbies. We also exchange tools and gift cards to buy tools for birthdays, Mother's/Father's Day, and Christmas.

Here are some other ideas to acquire farm and homestead tools.

- Gifts from family and friends (go ahead and ask for them!)
- Auctions and Estate Sales
- Yard Sales/Moving Sales (we love the "how much for the whole box" approach!)
- Family and friends downsizing (or upsizing and letting go of the old stuff!)
- Antique stores (a lot of times they don't even know what it is, or it looks awful but just needs a little WD-40!)
- Craigslist
- Regular Retailers (look for clearance bargains and coupons at Father's Day!)
- Amazon (I've found particularly good deals on name brand cordless pieces/sets at Christmas time!)

Where Do You Put What You Get?

Ugh! We talked about this in Chapter 3. This is a constant issue for us! Space to store, plus space to work is always a problem. We find ourselves moving equipment around constantly so that whatever needs work can be in the garage. But my dad worked in our open driveway with no cover for *years* before he could build a garage, so if you have a covered space, no matter what it is, be thankful!

Here are a couple points to think about when planning your shop space.

- **Think in phases.** An open carport can eventually be enclosed. A dirt floor can be graveled, a gravel floor can eventually be concreted. In the meantime, rubber mats on the floor will help and tarps across the open sides will keep some of the worse weather out.

- **Think about height.** Especially doors! A landscaping trailer doesn't need the height that an enclosed livestock or horse trailer needs. A tractor with a folding roll bar doesn't need the height of a non-folding bar or cab roof. But you still have to put it up and down before going in! High walls and ceilings give you room for loft storage space or for hanging things.

- **Think about width.** Again, especially doors! Our tractor with the disc on the back is wider than our truck. The fenders on our biggest trailer are also wider than the truck. And you want to be able to move around your equipment when you're inside to work on it!

- **Think about length.** Our longest trailer doesn't fit all the way in the garage. The tongue sticks out. Which means we can't lock the garage with the trailer inside. If you have the chance, size your building for your biggest equipment. Otherwise, the door must stay open at least a little bit.

- **Think about moisture.** Moisture can wreak havoc on your tools and equipment. Again, I don't have a great answer because this is something we still struggle with. Metal buildings are more affordable but have more condensation. But the more moisture-controlled your space is the more expensive it's going to be. Everything is a compromise.

There's a lot more to the homestead than just feeding the animals and building new pens and shelters. I'd say that repair and maintenance are more than 60% of how we spend our time. It's a full-time job to keep what you build and use in good working order!

****

CHAPTER EIGHT: ORGANIZING YOUR FARM RECORDS

Following that last chapter and thinking about all the maintenance that's required around here I am so glad that we've worked out a maintenance record-keeping system that is quick, easy, and efficient. Keeping up with maintenance is a key part of keeping your costs down. It's better to maintain it than have to replace it! And you certainly don't want to waste time and money buying the wrong parts or doubling up on maintenance work because you can't remember if, when, or how you did it last time.

We've developed a system for using Google Calendar to track certain important information and events in our farm management. Over the years it's even become a quick farm journal for us--backed up by paper and digital records of course! But using Google Calendar means that with a cell phone or tablet we have the critical information right at our fingertips in just moments, no matter where we are.

And honestly, this system could be useful for most of your home management records, whether you're farming or not!

Why Use a Digital Calendar Instead of Spreadsheets or Paper?

Well, first off, I think you can use any reasonable calendar app. Google is free, so that works for me. It's also available for any device and accessible with a web sign-in on any device and backed up to the Cloud. So, no worries if you have to replace your cell phone or your tablet dies. But you can also use Microsoft Outlook the same way. I'm sure there's also other apps that would do it, but I use those two every day and know they function basically the same in this use.

But why use a calendar app at all? Why not spreadsheets or more detailed farm management tools or paperwork? It is quick, easy, free, and can accomplish a large percentage of what a small farm or homestead might need. It hasn't replaced all our paper files, but I find the more we use it, the more we use it.

- It automatically tracks the date and time with each entry without extra notations.
- It allows you to add as much or as little information on the item as you want.

- Information can be added *immediately* so it's not forgotten or lost.
- You can go back and add items, events, or information later.
- It's completely searchable in moments, wherever you are.
- It can be shared by multiple users across multiple devices.
- Google is available on all technology platforms. (iOS, Android, etc.)
- You can set reminders and recurring appointments. (A huge help for routine maintenance!)
- You can print and save the information for later.
- You can attach documents to the calendar event to keep even more details all in one place.

What Farm Information Can You Track Using Google Calendar?

Here's a sample list of the things we use it for, and I'm sure there's more!

- Maintenance and repair of vehicles
- Maintenance and repair of equipment, tractors, and trailers
- Inspection, registration, licensing, and other fees on vehicles and equipment
- Tax payments, insurance payments and policy dates
- Large equipment, feed, or livestock purchases, sales, deliveries and/or pick-ups
- Routine livestock care like worming, vaccines, shearing, hoof trimming, etc.
- Breeding schedules, including exposure days, gestation calculations, and estimating lambing schedules
- Vet visits
- Major weather events like tropical storms, hurricanes, or nor'easters
- Major pasture rotations
- Major building maintenance project like painting or re-shingling
- Large tool, equipment, or appliance purchases for warranties

Most of these items will have critical associated paperwork, like invoices or receipts and using a digital calendar will not replace the need to have a safe place to file the paperwork. We use simple filing baskets under our computer desk to hold about 2 years at a time--then records are transferred to our regular home office filing cabinets. But the calendar app on your smartphone or tablet lets you have a quick summary of information at your fingertips. And if you have a bad habit of not getting caught up on your filing until tax time...well...you still have what you need!

How Do You Track Farm Records in Google Calendar?

Here's the nuts and bolts of the process, and why I said we've worked out a system. The functionality for you, as the farmer, is really based on the search features, so it deserves a little forethought if you want it to really be efficient for you.

1. **Create a new event.** You can do this either by double clicking in the date you want to add the event to, or clicking the red CREATE button.

2. **Enter the info you want to have available.** Think about what is *searchable* and what is *helpful*. Searchable is about choosing key words that you will remember *later*. Helpful what is the info you're most likely to need if you're at the part store or County tax office, on the tractor in the field, or talking to the repair shop or insurance agent on the phone. What stuff would you need to know and go find in your paperwork? Fill in that stuff!

3. **Add Reoccurring events as reminders.** If you click "Repeat" you can set up a reoccurring event to schedule things for yourself like oil changes, sheep worming, payments, vehicle inspections, vehicle tag renewals, and pet vaccinations.

4. **Add Organizational Details.** Depending on how much you use your calendar you can use color-coding, add attachments, and schedule reminders for yourself. I use reminders ("notification") more than anything else. I have also started using my phone to snap pictures of receipts, part boxes and numbers, or ear tags to remind myself. These pictures can be attached to your event and notes in Google Calendar.

After you've done it once or twice, it doesn't even take a whole minute to add an event to your calendar. And with a smartphone, you can add it right where you are--so I can add info into a repair note while in the garage looking at the parts box. I can add an oil change and grab the mileage while standing in the driveway waiting for the oil to drain. It's super convenient.

How Do You Use the SEARCH Feature in Google Calendar?

The search feature is the key to making this tool efficient for farm records. You type in your search keyword, and every "event" that you've created with that keyword comes up in chronological order. In seconds. Then you double-click the one you want and whatever you entered is right there.

Want to know if you're shearing earlier or later than two years ago? Search "sheep" or "shearing" and BAM, there it is. What to know how old the tires on the farm truck are because it feels like you *just* replaced them? I would search "GMC" and all the maintenance records for our GMC farm truck would pop up by date. Can't remember if you changed the air filter last time you did an oil change in the tractor? I can look that up in 3 clicks while we're at the parts counter.

But to make it that easy, we had to develop a bit more of a systematic approach. Who knew we would own 3 different "Dodge Trucks" in the span of 12 years? Confusion and over-generalization reduce the value of the tool. You must spend more time searching through your results to find which one you need.

Here are a few simple tips we implemented to make it work well for our small enterprise.

- **Title maintenance and repair entries with the YEAR, MAKE, and MODEL, or livestock type.** Don't title the entry using the action or type of repair. You don't want to search for "oil change" and have the oil change records for every tractor, vehicle, and ATV on the farm pop up. You want to search "2012 Dodge Ram" and have only the records for that truck come up, then skim for oil changes.

- **Note the business name of where repairs were done.** Including if it was at home. That way you know who to contact for follow up issues, warranties, or corrections.

- **Note mileage or working hours when adding maintenance and repair records.** Then you can track your part lifespans and match to product warranties as needed.

- **Detail which side/section/portion of work was done.** Such as "passenger side" or "exhaust from header to first joint." Put as much information as you can so that you decipher later if you're doing a repeat repair. This is also very important for animal records. You want to specify "right front hoof was significantly more overgrown than others" so that you can be sure to check it again next time.

- **Note where parts or supplies were purchase.** That way you can return them or return to that dealer to buy them again.

- **Note part numbers.** This is not necessary for everything, but certainly for any parts which tend to be difficult to find or often provided by mistake.

- **Title livestock events with the name of EACH SPECIES.** Just like with vehicles, title with the type of animal, not the action. Put the action in the notes section.

- **Go back and add check #s and payment dates.** This is particularly helpful if you're at a business office and need to refer to it. Tax payments, insurance payments, rental payments, even if you keep the receipt you never know when you'll need to refer to that payment info and not have your filing cabinet handy.

A quick word about using multiple separate calendars...

There is great functionality in Google and Outlook to create multiple separate and individual calendars and then layer them together. I use it to keep our family calendar separate from my off- farm job calendar. This can also be a way to keep multiple family members synched.

But it can get confusing fast and there's always the chance that you'll enter an event in the wrong calendar and then not be able to find it later--been there, done that! We've reduced our system to a work calendar for me and a home calendar for everything farm, home, and kids. We use a *very simple* color-coding system to differentiate. Green for all things home, farm, and animals. Blue for all things imported from my work calendar. Red for payments. We use a paper calendar in the kitchen for all the daily family activities and events other than birthdays. (I use reoccurring appointments in Google for birthday reminders!)

****

CHAPTER 9: FINDING UNEXPECTED GOODNESS ON THE FARM

Farming is a lot of work.

A lot of sweat and heartache and a lot of tough decisions to be made, almost all the time. You get caught in the hustle and bustle and if you're not careful you'll miss the things that are right in front of you. You're so focused on the future, the next thing on the list, the next event coming up...you start to miss the moments right under your nose—then suddenly farming is an ugly thing.

But I find that my phone is full of snapshots that say it isn't ugly. Between all the sweat and scrubbing and hauling and worrying and working, there's precious moments in there that can't be replace by any other lifestyle.

Moments like sitting on an overturned 5-gallon bucket and listening to the chicks peep, peep, peep with their momma. Watching them learn to scratch and shuffle through the grass and listening to her deep cluck and coo as she pulled them all in underneath her for the night.

Moments like sitting on a log and watching the dogs swim and splash through a mucky pond. Hearing the frogs go silent, then the plop, plop, plop as they all dive for cover as the dogs come near.

The moment when a bull calf turns and watches you, curiously, through the green pasture with a backdrop of droning bugs--not sure if he should run from the dogs or trust in the electric fence.

The moment when a warm breeze blows your sweaty hair off your neck while you're picking tomatoes...when you see a clump of wildflowers along the fence line...when you actually recognize the mockingbird's song in the walnut tree because it's the same every morning at 6:54 am...seeing dragonflies lined up along the fence wire...the earthy smell of damp sheep in the heavy morning dew...the sparkle of clean water in a freshly scrubbed trough...

It's important to take time to find these moments in between all the work that farming takes to help you remember your purpose, your goals, and the sweetness of the small farm or homestead life that you've chosen. T

Those moments are what make it worth it when the checkbook balances say otherwise!

****

REFERENCES

1. *You Can Farm: The Entrepreneur's Guide to Start and Succeed in a Farming Enterprise*, by Joel Salatin. 1998.

2. *Pastured Poultry Profits*, by Joel Salatin. 1996.

3. *Small-Scale Livestock Farming: A Grass-Based Approach for Health, Sustainability, and Profit*, by Carol Ekarius. 1999.

4. *Barnyard in Your Backyard: A Beginners Guide to Raising Chickens, Ducks, Geese, Rabbits, Goats, Sheep, and Cattle*, by Gail Damerow. 2002.

5. *The Backyard Homestead Guide to Raising Farm Animals*, by Gail Damerow. 2011.

6. *Quality Pasture: How to Create it, Manage It, and Profit from It*, by Allan Nation. 1995.

7. *Pasture Perfect: How You Can Benefit from Choosing Meat, Eggs, and Dairy Products from Grass Fed Animals*, by Jo Robinson. 2004.

8. *All Flesh is Grass: The Pleasures and Promises of Pasture Farming*, by Gene Logsdon. 2004.

Direct links for Reference items can be found at
https://www.walkinginhighcotton.net/dollars-and-cents-resources/

WORKSHEETS

1. Finding Land for Your Small Farm

2. Assessing Land and Community Around Your Small Farm

3. Buildings and Shelters for Your Small Farm

4. When to Call the Vet at Your Small Farm

5. Farm Visit Notes

6. Choosing Livestock for Your Small Farm

7. Assessing Livestock Breeds for Your Small Farm

The Dollars and Cents of Starting Your Small Farm or Homestead

Finding Land for Your Small Farm

What does my PERFECT farm property look like?

What features are critical for having animals?

What features do I want that can NOT be added later?

What features do I think I could realistically add later?

What are deal-breakers that I should walk away from?

The Dollars and Cents of Starting Your Small Farm or Homestead

Assessing Land and Community

Is this area rural, suburban, urban, or fringe?

What feed and implement stores are nearby?

What is the property's existing zoning district?

What other types of farms are in the area?

What is the zoning of adjacent and nearby land?

Where are the nearest large animal vet clinics?

What is the future land use plan for the property and adjacent areas.

What is my access to or responsibility for providing roads, water, and septic?

The Dollars and Cents of Starting Your Small Farm or Homestead

Buildings and Shelters

- What is the buildings purpose? What do I need to store or shelter?

- Does it need to be, or can it be, mobile?

- What am I using for storage now? Will this match my current need, use, and work patterns?

- Can this building, in this location, be expanded in the future?

- Is this the most practical and cost efficient option? What are future maintenance requirements?

- Do I have materials onsite that can be used or repurposed for this project?

- Is this the right location? Am I sure? Have I used this location temporarily to be sure?

- Does it matter how it looks? Will the general public be able to see it? Will I be able to see it from my house?

The Dollars and Cents of Starting Your Small Farm or Homestead

WHEN TO CALL THE VET

IS THE ANIMAL SICK?

I DON'T KNOW?!?

↓

Watch and Wait. Re-assess in 24 hours.

Yes. We got this. Maybe a phone call to the vet or a neighbor to help us along.

YEP. Definitely something wrong here!

↓

Have we seen or dealt with this before?

↓

No. This is all new to us.

↓

Can we afford *at least* $300 for a farm call?

↓

Does the animal have a 50/50 chance at survival?

↓

Does the animal have a 50/50 chance to be productive on the farm again?

↓

Is there a chance this is contagious and will spread? Or be transmitted to humans?

↓

Is there a chance this could come up again and we could save money in the future by knowing how to treat it ourselves?

YES → **Call the Vet**

For Personal Use ONLY © Walking in High Cotton

The Dollars and Cents of Starting Your Small Farm or Homestead

Farm Visit Notes

Farm Name: _____

Address/Location: _____
_____

Season of Visit: _____

Weather During Visit: _____

Years in Operation: _____

Type of Operation: _____

Other General Notes:

Their general environment...terrain, climate, forested areas?

MY general environment?

Their mission...purpose, values, key products?

MY mission?

Their operating system...major inputs, equipment usage, labor usage, key operational tasks?

MY main operating system?

For Personal Use ONLY © Walking in High Cotton

The Dollars and Cents of Starting Your Small Farm or Homestead

Choosing Livestock for Your Farm

What foods do I eat that I could produce? What livestock produces that food?

What non-meat products do I use that I could produce? What livestock produces that item?

What foods do I think there is a market to sell? What livestock produces that food?

What non-meat products do I think I have a market to sell? What livestock produces that item?

What livestock will fit in the shelters and pastures I already have on site? What can I afford to build?

Am I ready to provide health care, first aid, and nurse sick animals? Do I have a network of experts or community connections to help me?

How much time and energy do I have to commit to daily care?

Do I have the knowledge and physical strength to handle livestock? What limitations do I have?

For Personal Use ONLY © Walking in High Cotton

The Dollars and Cents of Starting Your Small Farm or Homestead

Assessing Livestock BREEDS

MY FARM ENVIRONMENT & OPERATING SYSTEM

KEY TRAITS I'M LOOKING FOR IN MY LIVESTOCK

BREED: _____

Key Traits of This Breed

What are the food/water/shelter requirements for this breed? Any key or unusual care traits?

What are the routine health needs for this species? Any key or unusual health traits?

What products can I get from this breed? What specialty markets might apply with this breed?

Where can I get these animals? Is there a dependable supply of breeding and replacement stock?

For Personal Use ONLY © Walking in High Cotton

www.ingramcontent.com/pod-product-compliance
Lightning Source LLC
Chambersburg PA
CBHW081057240526
45465CB00025B/2514